Meals at Midnight

Meals at Midnight

Poems

Michael McClintock

*For Larry Smith,
author of Lake Winds, in
Friendship
Michael
McClintock
Nov. 2014*

MODERN ENGLISH TANKA PRESS
BALTIMORE, MARYLAND
2008

THE UNEXAMINED LIFE IS NOT WORTH LIVING.
SOCRATES

MODERN ENGLISH TANKA PRESS
P.O. Box 43717
Baltimore, Maryland 21236 USA

www.modernenglishtankapress.com
publisher@modernenglishtankapress.com

Meals at Midnight
Copyright © 2008 by Michael McClintock.
All rights reserved.

Cover Art "Mistress of Butterflies" Copyright © 2008
by Michael McClintock.

Acknowledgements
Grateful acknowledgement is made to the following publications
in which these poems first appeared:
American Tanka,
Blithe Spirit: Journal of the British Haiku Society [U.K.],
Bottle Rockets, Eucalypt [Australia], *Gusts* [Canada],
Hermitage [Romania],
The Heron's Nest, Kokako [N.Z.],
Modern English Tanka, Modern Haiku,
Moonset, Presence [U.K.],
Ribbons: Tanka Society of America Journal,
Santa Fe Broadsides,
Tanka Splendor, Wisteria, and *Writer's Digest.*

Printed in the United States of America, 2008.

ISBN 1-935398-01-6

For my wife, Karen

Nunc et semper.

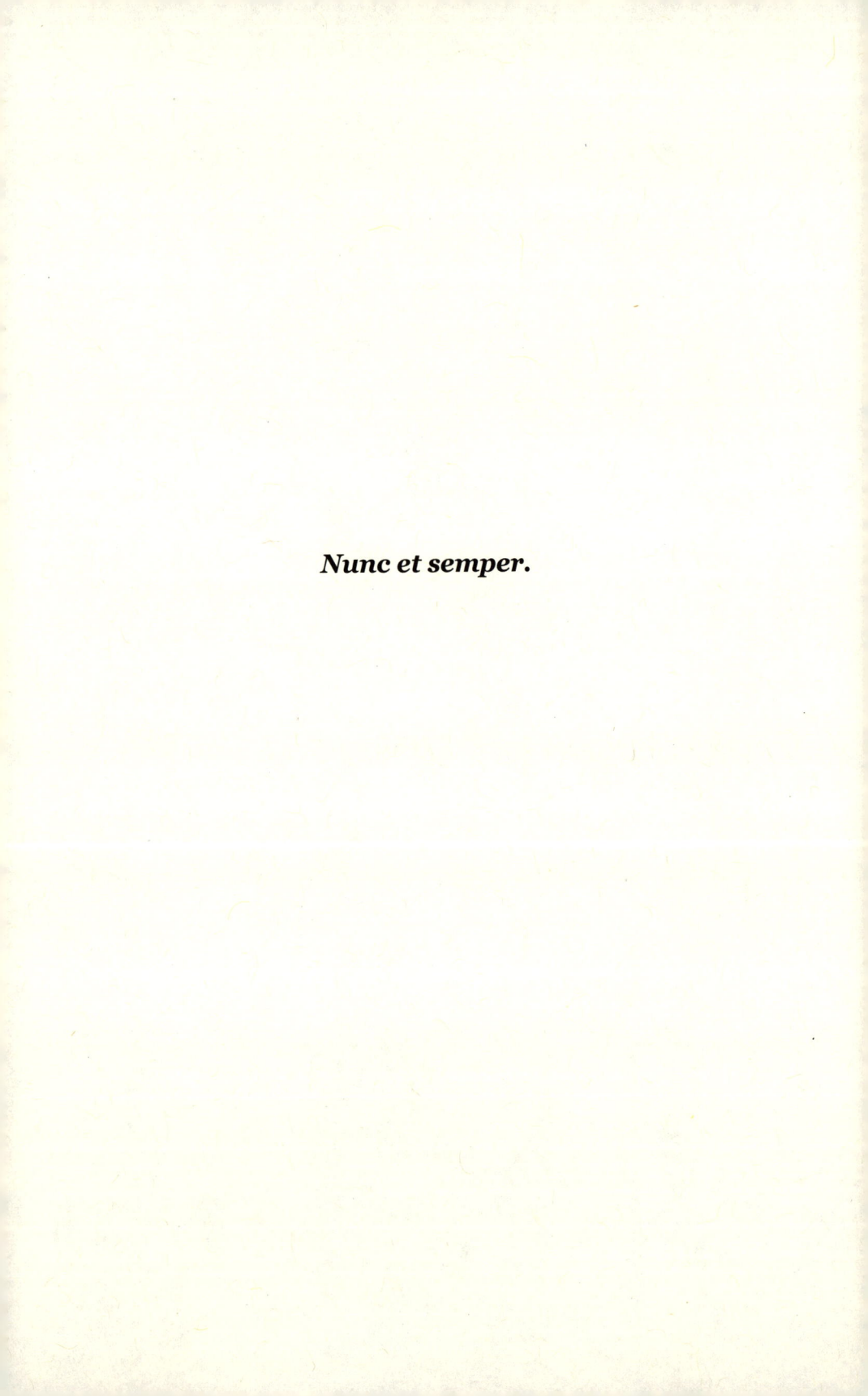

Contents

I. The Enormous Sea, 7

II. Rinsing Peas, 23

III. The Evening Chill, 47

IV. Folding in for the Night, 73

Michael McClintock

I.

a long letter . . .
honeysuckle in the window
and the enormous sea

Michael McClintock

the day before
heading off to the Army,
my father and friends
smiling into the camera—
smart, funny, and immortal

Meals at Midnight

      digging up roots
      I find two
      folded like hands,
      deeper than the others,
      and re-bury them

Michael McClintock

looking off
toward a clamor of bells
in the distance—
I've a strong desire
to see you again

Meals at Midnight

inside
my candlelit tent
I've set up a mirror
and begun shaving
shadows from my face

Michael McClintock

kiln-dark,
heather-scented—
your eyes and hair bring spring
to the empty desert
place where I live

Meals at Midnight

        turning on the lamp,
        turning off the lamp:
        deciding
        what to do
        one April evening

Michael McClintock

reading Vergil
is my rest, the best time
that lucid hour
when the sun's a chariot
wheeling through the cedars

Meals at Midnight

        squelching through mud,
        out of the valley we climb,
        hunting mushrooms—
        our dispute abandoned
        to that single purpose

Michael McClintock

from my hill
I watch you pick up and re-read
the letter I left you
in that secret place we promised
never again to visit

Meals at Midnight

                        from the wind of heaven
              ready to rest—
        grateful,
     I reel in
my dragon kite

Michael McClintock

the warbler singing
over there in the plum tree—
so clear a voice
it must have drunk very deeply
at some pool freshened by rain

Meals at Midnight

        old ruins
        on the edge of town
        weighted in leaves . . .
        the wisteria flourishes
        there especially, in spring

Michael McClintock

the new calendar
hanging on the office wall
above the gossip:
    green pagodas
    shrouded in fog

Michael McClintock

II.

July heat . . .
rinsing peas in water
cold from the well

Michael McClintock

following a route
of many twists and turns
a butterfly joins me
for rest within the sanctuary
at the edge of the windy field

Meals at Midnight

beginning
with a lump of clay
wet with spit
my fingers shape
a rain goddess

Michael McClintock

in the world
outside the office window
a cloud
detaches from the others
and enters my dream

Meals at Midnight

        forty miles
        of bad road—
        at the end,
        a small town green with trees
        where every woman is beautiful

Michael McClintock

early at my door,
the star of morning
in your eyes—
of course I will do anything
you want me to do today

Meals at Midnight

in warm weather
after darkness falls
building a fire
just big enough to light
our faces for conversation

Michael McClintock

leaving a warm bed
to write the lines that come
before sleep—
I hold my face to the rain
falling from another world

Meals at Midnight

        one at a time,
        I step on stones
        and cross the stream—
        when I'm across, the stones
        go back to what they were doing

Michael McClintock

four lines deep
into the first poem
of the day—I pause
airing my white whiskers
in the morning coolness

Meals at Midnight

like a bee I need
the scent of honey—
you've been gone
and I've been crawling
into your bed for naps

Michael McClintock

summer days
long and hot like this one
I live outside
a friend of green shadows
and the sycamore tree

Meals at Midnight

there's a house
far back in the summer woods
I've visited for years . . .
a noon-hour nap is still
my only way to get there

Michael McClintock

selecting a flavor
I've never had before,
mango-orange—
that will be my mood today,
the hottest of the year

Meals at Midnight

        fresh for work,
        pants belted tight,
        head clear,
        I wade into the windblown
        foam of the morning prairie

Michael McClintock

stuck on a bus
crossing endless Nebraska,
too much on my mind—
ah, on the noon-bright wheat
the wind and its shadows

Meals at Midnight

when I listen to Haydn,
all the wishes I might make
glide into the sun
slow, like long-limbed dreamers
from the deep end of the woods

Michael McClintock

where do they hurry
at this hour of morning?
white butterflies—
not a shadow beneath them
on the sun-beaten grass

Meals at Midnight

        filling a bowl
        my mother made from river clay,
        the season's first cherries;
        I mist them with some water,
        so they'll sparkle a little

Michael McClintock

a few rubber bands
to hold up my socks,
I wade the shallows
searching for the shoes I lost
playing Crusoe with the tide

Meals at Midnight

        it doesn't matter
        where the beach is, or how
        you get me there—
        lay me on a sheet of wind,
        like a sand mandala

Michael McClintock

with a kiss and shove,
the dream I'm waking from
sends me packing . . .
the feel of the ship turning
in a wide arc on the sea

Michael McClintock

III.

a little inn
with a swinging sign-board . . .
the evening chill

Michael McClintock

so long since
my boots were off
what am I
to say to my feet
when I see them?

Meals at Midnight

a bachelor bat
has made a home
inside the window shutter;
I welcome
quiet company

Michael McClintock

holy rites
softly spoken . . .
I lose the words
but my heart
knows the prayer

Meals at Midnight

        such was their power,
        I lost all sense of time,
        reading old poems . . .
        journeying into morning
        high in Chinese mountains

Michael McClintock

endless portraits
of the great poets
of long ago
appear in the clouds
billowing over Hunan

Meals at Midnight

a clear, cobalt sky,
and a boulder's worn hollow—
here's where I'll sit,
giving an hour to love
September emptiness

Michael McClintock

bent with age,
my neighbor the beekeeper—
what is it he does
working bare-headed and alone
among the tall sunflowers?

Meals at Midnight

        cleaning my closet
        I count eight raincoats
        finding enough room
        for eight more, in the years ahead,
        if I am very careful

Michael McClintock

washing rice—
I'm fond of that sound
at nightfall,
the wind huffing a little
past the kitchen's thin door

Meals at Midnight

straying
into the flower-market
our errand for shoes
brings home daffodils
wet from Belize

Michael McClintock

a fall afternoon
turned gusty—
the crackle of leaves
and everywhere, everywhere,
the smell of haylofts

Meals at Midnight

      admiring the oak
      and knowing, of course,
      I haven't the strength
      or roots, or simple desire
      to stand so long in one place

Michael McClintock

choices, choices
at the little shop
on the avenue—
for a friend who's faraway,
the card with the paper circus

Meals at Midnight

        tonight
        I'm going out to count
        the stars—
        if you wait up for me
        I might bring back a few

Michael McClintock

a wheelbarrow's purpose
this morning shall be
holding rainwater
so the clouds have a place
to come and go as they like

Meals at Midnight

where the sun rises
and where it sets—
the things I learn first
in each place I come to live,
making my home between them

Michael McClintock

"Meet me tomorrow"
your love note said—
I tuck it away
in the old school notebook
and pour a large Scotch

Meals at Midnight

a small turn-out
for tonight's haiku reading—
the poet, his wife,
and a cricket chirping
to the moon at the door

Michael McClintock

the wind
crackling the leaves—
there's nothing
like opening a window
awhile to listen

Meals at Midnight

        dividing pecans
        one for you, one for me
        out of a basket—
        powers and realities
        that make unshakeable sense

Michael McClintock

the way it looks
like a dragon fallen
from the sky,
this uprooted tree
alone on the moor

Meals at Midnight

        black skimmers
        whir over the lake,
        back to their island;
        I am where I am
        in the long twilight

Michael McClintock

the moonlit cedars,
an owl or two—
I'd like to stay up all night
but I've work for tomorrow
and days grow short

Michael McClintock

IV.

winter rain . . .
pigeons under a bridge
folding in for the night

Michael McClintock

at the center
of Manhattan
a manhole cover
catches the rain
and makes it swirl

Meals at Midnight

wanting to go
into my room
and be alone, yet
leaving the door
open a crack

Michael McClintock

downloading the movie
"The Martians Attack"
from a satellite—
a moment to wonder who else
may be watching tonight

Meals at Midnight

        my love whistles
        a light-hearted ditty,
        baking shrimp
        for our meal at midnight—
        because sometimes we must eat

Michael McClintock

early snow . . .
from islands of the north,
ice-packed bonito;
since summer I have waited
to hear the fish-monger's call!

Meals at Midnight

      the best road
      from my house to yours
      is a frozen creek
      engineered by water alone
      without a day's labor

Michael McClintock

right there
in the wide blue sky
above me:
that is where I find
the origin of loneliness

Meals at Midnight

                      in the woods nearby
                      everything's blue and black—
                      those smallest of sounds
                      must be the coming night
                      counting her children

Michael McClintock

the Mona Lisa print
wears a beaded rainbow necklace
drawn in waxy crayon—
a small boy's desire
to make her less plain

Meals at Midnight

        tongue between teeth
        a child
        with new watercolors
        causing green elephants
        to be created

Michael McClintock

the mausoleum
and weeping willows
inside the old brooch—
slowly it dawns on me
they are made of hair

Meals at Midnight

carefully winding
a forkful of ramen
around a pea
tonight is the longest
night of the year

Michael McClintock

when alone
on a barge in the harbor
at midnight
I feel like the only
fool on earth

Meals at Midnight

Remembering Cid Corman

sun,
rock,
moon:

good friend
the language
you gave us
read,
heard,
received

Michael McClintock

just over
the ridge
that world
that goes on
forever

Meals at Midnight

        nursing a mouth
        full of aching teeth,
        well past midnight
        I close the book of poems
        about the solitude of mountains

Michael McClintock

sugar cane
lemon grass
green mustard
on this day of winter fog
the comfort of lists

Meals at Midnight

        with no plans
        for special celebration
        I rake up some leaves
        and repair the door-chimes
        this last day of the year

Michael McClintock

these thoughts
that come and go,
what are they really
but a glitter of light
on leaves and water

Biographical Note

Michael McClintock holds degrees from Occidental College and the University of Southern California in English and American Literature, Asian Studies, and Information Science. McClintock's poetry has been widely published and translated internationally, including by Nobel Laureate, Czeslaw Milosz. He resides in Los Angeles and Fresno, California, following a career as principal librarian, film and recordings curator, and administrator for the County of Los Angeles Public Library System.

Other Books by Michael McClintock

Collections:

Light Run (Shiloh, 1971)
Man With No Face (Shelters Press, 1974)
Maya (Seer Ox, 1976)
Anthology of Days (Backwoods Broadsides Chaplet Series No. 70, 2002)
Letters in Time: Sixty Short Poems (Hermitage West, 2005)
Sketches from the San Joaquin (Turtle Light Press, 2008).

Anthologies:

The Tanka Anthology with Pamela Miller Ness and Jim Kacian (Red Moon Press, 2003).

With Denis M. Garrison, from Modern English Tanka Press:

The Five-Hole Flute: Modern English Tanka in Sequences and Sets (2006)
The Dreaming Room: Modern English Tanka in Collage and Montage Sets (2007)
Landfall: Poetry of Place in Modern English Tanka (2007)
Streetlights: Poetry of Urban Life in Modern English Tanka (2009)

Also from MODERN ENGLISH TANKA PRESS
www.modernenglishtankapress.com www.themetpress.com

Lilacs After Winter • Francis Masat

Proposing to the Woman in the Rear View Mirror • James Tipton

Abacus: Prose poems, haibun and short poems • Gary LeBel

Looking for a Prince: a collection of senryu and kyoka • Alexis Rotella

The Tanka Prose Anthology • Jeffrey Woodward, Ed.

Greetings from Luna Park • Sedoka by James Roderick Burns

In Two Minds • Responsive Tanka by Amelia Fielden and Kathy Kituai

An Unknown Road • Haiku by Adelaide B. Shaw

Slow Motion: The Log of a Chesapeake Skipjack • M. Kei

Ash Moon Anthology: Poems on Aging in Modern English Tanka • Alexis Rotella & Denis M. Garrison, Eds.

Fire Blossoms: The Birth of Haiku Noir • Denis M. Garrison

Cigarette Butts and Lilacs: tokens of a heritage • Tanka by Andrew Riutta

Sailor in the Rain and Other Poems • Denis M. Garrison

Four Decades on My Tanka Road: Tanka Collections of Sanford Goldstein • Sanford Goldstein. Fran Witham, Ed.

this hunger, tissue-thin: new & selected tanka 1995-2005 • Larry Kimmel

Jun Fujita, Tanka Pioneer • Denis M. Garrison, Ed.

Landfall: Poetry of Place in Modern English Tanka • Denis M. Garrison and Michael McClintock, Eds.

Lip Prints: Tanka and Other Short Poems 1979-2007 • Alexis Rotella

Ouch: Senryu That Bite • Alexis Rotella

Eavesdropping: Seasonal Haiku • Alexis Rotella

Tanka Teachers Guide • Denis M. Garrison, Ed.

Five Lines Down: A Landmark in English Tanka • Denis M. Garrison, Ed.

Sixty Sunflowers: TSA Members' Anthology 2006-2007 • Sanford Goldstein, Ed.

The Dreaming Room: Modern English Tanka in Collage and Montage Sets • Michael McClintock and Denis M. Garrison, Eds.

Haiku Harvest 2000-2006 • Denis M. Garrison, Ed.

Eight Shades of Blue • Haiku by Denis M. Garrison

The Salesman's Shoes • Tanka by James Roderick Burns

Hidden River • Haiku by Denis M. Garrison

The Five-Hole Flute: Modern English Tanka in Sequences and Sets • Denis M. Garrison and Michael McClintock, Eds.

Journals • *Modern English Tanka* •
• *Atlas Poetica* • *Modern Haiga* •
• *Ambrosia* • *Prune Juice* •